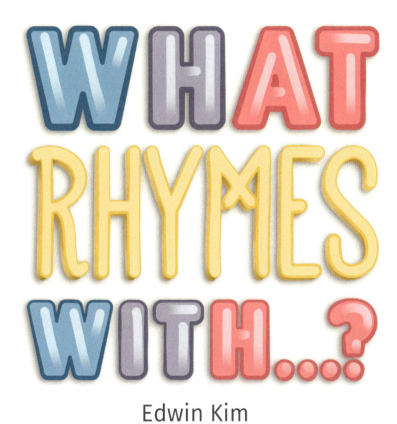

Edwin Kim

COPYRIGHT © ASCEND DIGITAL
ALL RIGHTS RESERVED

Get ready to start your adventure in the land of rhymes. Relax, find a comfy spot, you might find some words that rhyme a lot!

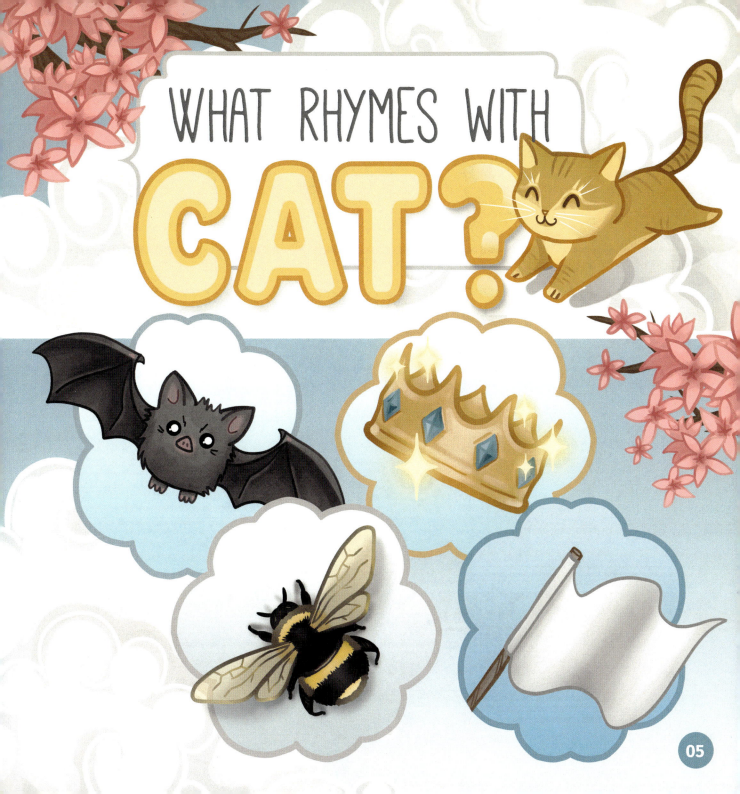

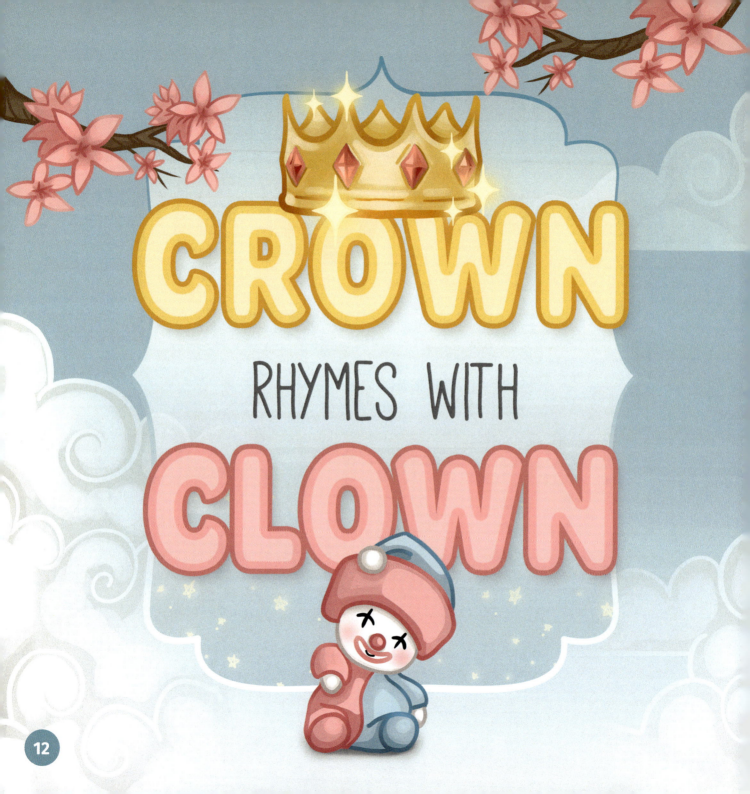

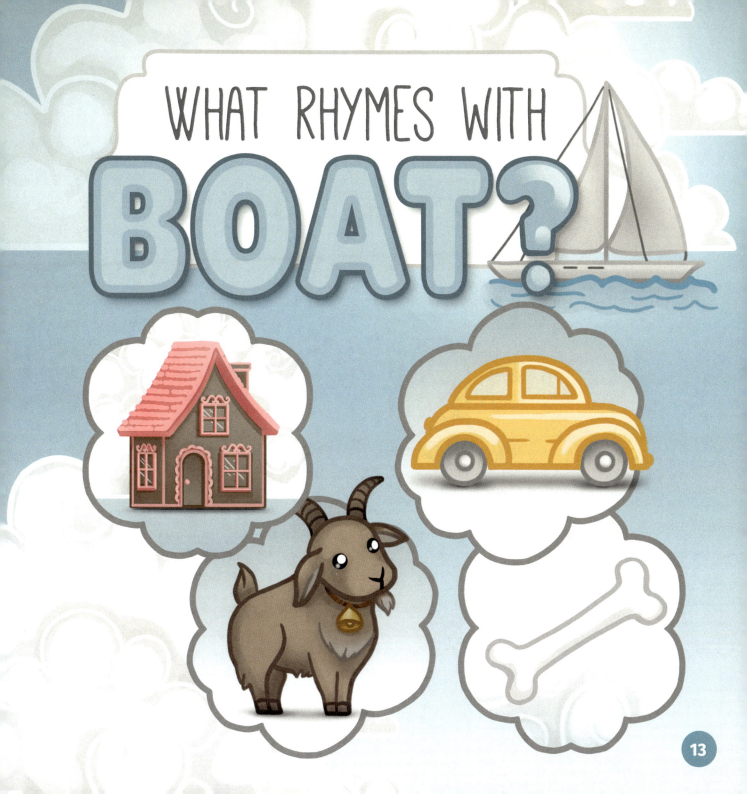

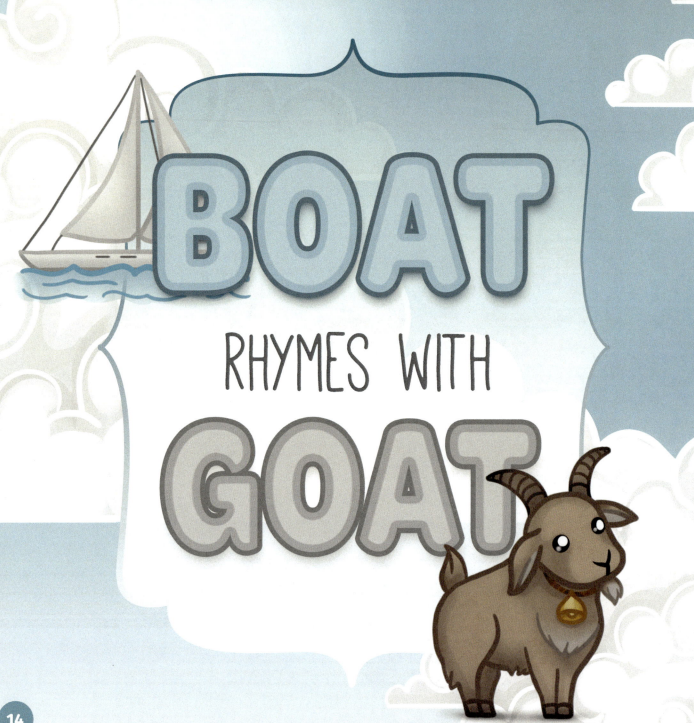

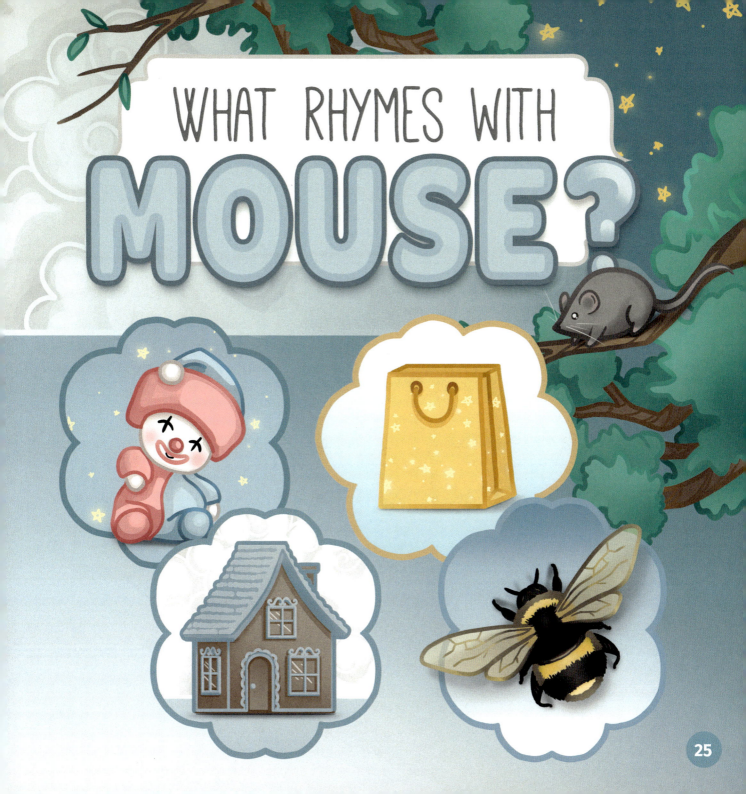

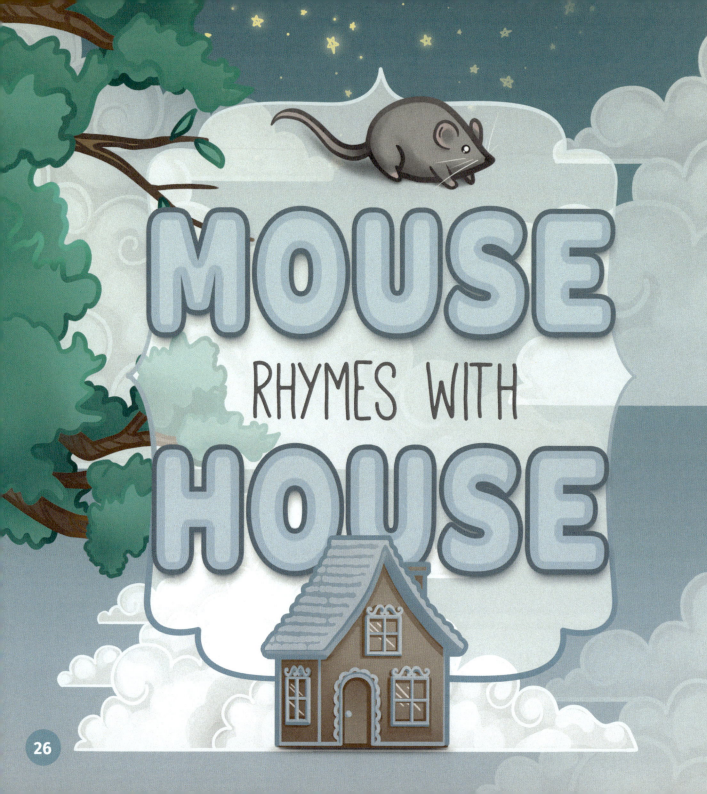

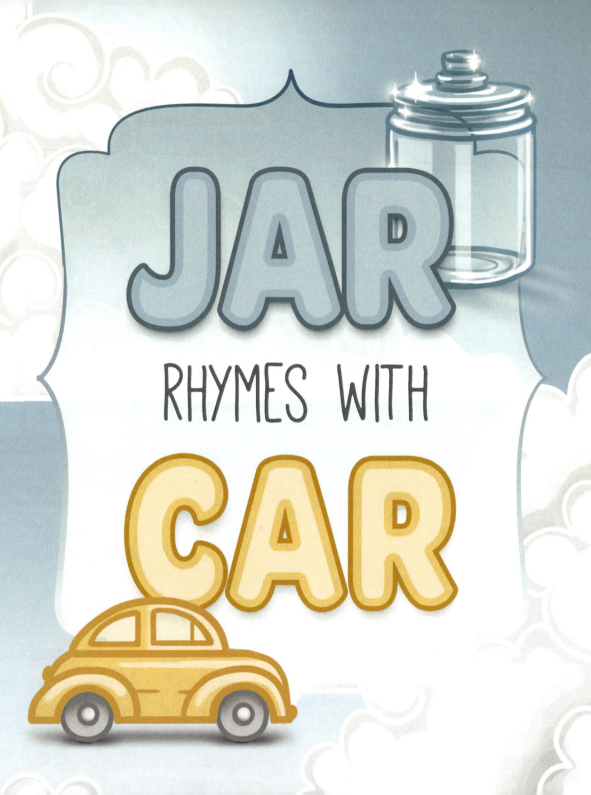

JAR
RHYMES WITH
CAR

MOON

RHYMES WITH

SPOON

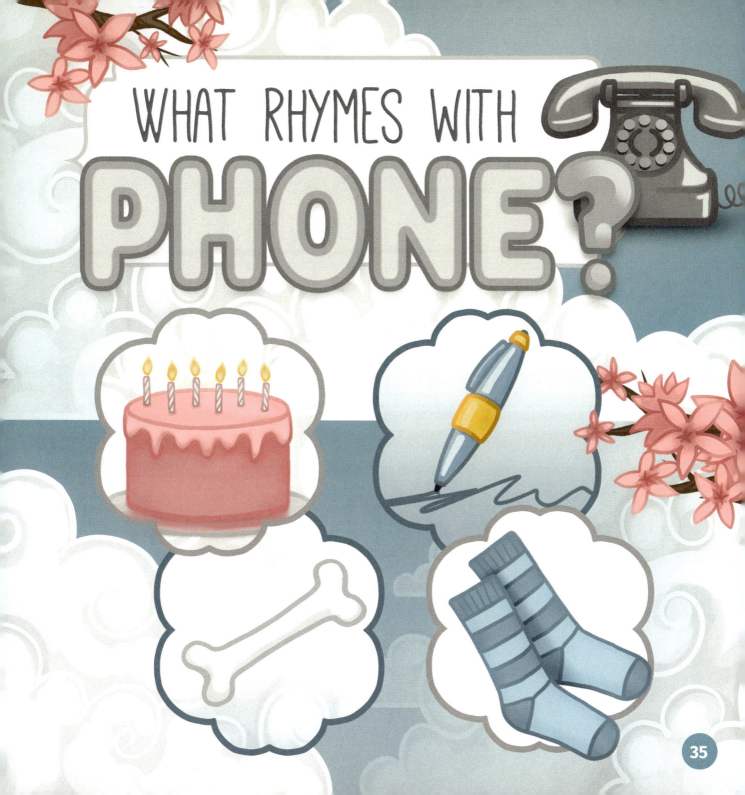

BAG RHYMES WITH FLAG

Made in the USA
Monee, IL
03 October 2021